KEEPSAKE CRAFTS

CHRISTMAS TREE
DECORATIONS

KEEPSAKE CRAFTS

CHRISTMAS TREE DECORATIONS

DEBORAH SCHNEEBELI-MORRELL

SUNSET PUBLISHING CORPORATION
MENLO PARK, CALIFORNIA

A QUARTO BOOK

First Printing June 1995

Copyright © 1995 Quarto Inc.
Published by Sunset Publishing Corporation,
Menlo Park, CA 94025

ISBN 0-376-04262-1

Library of Congress Catalog Card Number:
94-068456

For more information on Keepsake Crafts
Christmas Tree Decorations or any other
Sunset Book, call 1-800-634-3095.

This book was designed and produced by
Quarto Inc.
6 Blundell St,
London N7 9BH

Editor Joanne Jessop
Managing editor Anna Clarkson
Designers Peter Bridgewater/
Ron Bryant-Funnell
Photographer Heini Schneebeli
Illustrator Tony Masero
Art director Moira Clinch
Editorial director Sophie Collins

Manufactured in Hong Kong by
Regent Publishing Services Ltd
Printed in China by
Leefung-Asco Printers Ltd

CONTENTS

INTRODUCTION

Christmas is a special, magical celebration that helps to lift our spirits during the darkest time of the year. In almost every home the Christmas tree, with its ornaments and dazzling lights, becomes the focal point, creating a festive atmosphere that delights adults and children alike.

But shopping for decorations that suit your personal tastes and match your home decor is not an easy task, especially during the busy holiday season. It is much more rewarding to create your own special decorations. With the help of the

inspiring and inventive ideas presented in this book, you can decorate your Christmas tree in your own unique style. Have friends and family join in these projects to make Christmas a special time of quiet enjoyment and togetherness.

The projects in this book draw their inspiration from a rich variety of sources – from the traditional world of folk crafts to more elegant and exotic sources. The materials, too, are varied and interesting to work with. Metal foils, glittering glass beads, old bits of jewelry, and scraps of colorful fabric will add sparkle and shine to

your Christmas tree decorations.
Sometimes, when working with flowers
or shells, the natural beauty of the
materials themselves will inspire the
design. In other projects, some very
ordinary household objects, such as
scouring pads, are put to extraordinary
uses with stunning results.

These festive Christmas tree
decorations could become treasured
additions to your family collection or
lovely gifts with a personal touch.

MATERIALS

Many of the projects in this book have been inspired by the exciting and inventive work of folk artists from less technically sophisticated cultures than our own. The book aims to encourage the reader to be resourceful, to be inspired by everyday objects and to transform ordinary materials into lovely and unusual decorations. It is a good idea to build up a rich and varied collection of materials; to some extent the availability of materials will dictate your style and, therefore, how your work will look. Many of the materials used in this book are quite readily available, either from a notions department, art suppliers, or even your own collection of discarded items – nothing is more rewarding than recycling throwaway objects into beautiful and useful things. Hobby or bead shops have an amazing choice of products from all over the world, as well as wire and thread.

Once you have gathered enough simple materials for a

few of the projects, let your imagination loose and enjoy yourself, while discovering new ways of using materials and simple techniques.

METAL FOIL

The metal foil used for the repoussé work in the first six projects is really the only material that needs to be bought from a special source, such as a sheet metal supplier, although some may be available from good craft or art stores. Kitchen aluminum foil is much too thin, but if you do have difficulties finding the right metal foil, aluminum take-out or frozen food containers could be used. Another substitute is opened-up aluminum soft-drink cans – but always be careful when cutting metal and beware of sharp corners.

FABRIC AND RIBBONS

The fabric projects all use small scraps of quite vivid and lustrous materials saved from dressmaking, cut from old clothes, or even found in a dress-up box. The effect of appliquéd contrasting fabric with simple sequined and beaded embroidery is quite stunning, especially when crowned with brightly colored feathers plucked deftly from a clean feather duster (see Embroidered Birds on page 24).

Short lengths of exotic ribbon, brightly colored or luxuriant to the touch, can have stunning effects and are inexpensive to buy in very small quantities.

For Embroidered Birds (page 24), Sparkling Stars and Precious Parcels (page 26), and Luscious Leaves & Flowers (page 28), small amounts of polyester padding were used to stuff the decorations. You could also use nylon stockings or pantyhose.

BUTTONS AND BEADS

Nearly every household has some small tins and boxes, perhaps hidden at the back of a drawer, containing old buttons and beads. Supplement this collection with a variety of new buttons and beads of all shapes and sizes, made from colored glass, plastic crystals, teardrop pearls, little seed beads, and pressed metal charms. Always look out for exciting and unusual items when you are shopping, even if you are not making anything in particular at the time; you never know when you will need something really special.

JEWELS

Old or unwanted cheap jewelry is a good way of making a tree decoration look particularly exotic and resplendent. Look for old jewelry in junk shops or at rummage sales; a good notions department may sell flat-backed jewels. The miniature mirrors used on page 20 come from a dolls' house shop.

PAPIER-MÂCHÉ

Papier-mâché pulp is a very versatile medium that was used to model Frosted Fruit (page 29), Brilliant Birds (page 30) and Little Painted Animals (page 32). It has also been used as a backing for Dazzling Dangles (page 42), as well as Tree Topper (pages 62-3). Pulp mix is widely available from craft or toy stores, and is inexpensive when used in small quantities. However, you may want to make your own pulp, especially if you enjoy working in this medium. The recipe is on page 29.

PAPERS AND WRAPPINGS

A wide variety of brightly colored papers, glittery candy wrappers, colored tissue paper, and hand-printed Indian papers has been used in the découpage-inspired projects, Ornaments Galore (page 38) and the glittering faceted star in Tree Toppers (page 62). Build up your own supply by saving gift wrap, chocolate or Easter egg wrappers, and anything that catches your eye; it may be just what you need some day.

NATURAL ITEMS

If you go for walks in the woods, fields, or along the beach, don't miss the chance to collect unusual items. Seeds, pine cones, shells, and poppy seed heads are all used in Shell Ornaments (page 48) and Nuts & Seeds (page 50). Those you can't find, you can buy from specialty shops.

GLUES, PAINTS, AND VARNISH

Four different types of glues are used in this book, and all are easily available – white glue, clear glue, epoxy glue, and a cellulose paste for the découpage projects.

The paints used in these projects are all acrylic or gouache. Both are water based and both dry quickly to an opaque finish that doesn't run. Polyurethane varnish is used in Salt Dough (page 54).

BASIC TECHNIQUES

All the projects provide guidelines and practical tips for creating stunning decorations. But this is only the beginning in each case there are endless possibilities to be explored. The aim of this book is to spark your creative talents and encourage you to experiment with other techniques and materials to invent your own personal designs.

No special technical ability is necessary for these projects, and they can all be made at home using simple everyday tools. Many projects use leftover materials such as candy wrappers and old newspapers that you might have saved.

I For the sewing projects you can use scraps of fabric, ribbons, buttons, sequins, and brightly colored feathers plucked from a feather duster. You need only the most rudimentary sewing and embroidery skills. The success and quality of the decorations lies not so much in the skill of the maker but more in the clever and inventive use of materials.

2 For some projects, particularly the repoussé metal decorations and the painted tin animals, you will need sheet metal foil from a good craft store or sheet metal supplier. These materials are surprisingly easy to work with. The metal is thin and cuts easily with scissors.

3 You can even draw on it, or trace designs from this book if you do not feel confident in your own drawing skills.

4 Papier-mâché pulp is used in several projects. You can use a ready-made paper pulp or make your own from the recipe on page 29.

5 Some projects require simple craft techniques that most people have tried, such as découpage, painting, and modeling in papier-mâché.

6 Nimble fingers and a little patience are all that are needed for the simpler projects such as the pomanders. And what could be simpler than tying bows and stringing beads together?

REPOUSSÉ METAL SHAPES

The stunning effect of these lovely glittering metal ornaments belies the simplicity of making them.

This lightweight metal foil is thin enough to be cut with an ordinary pair of scissors; the relief of repoussé work is created by drawing on the back of the metal with a dry ballpoint pen. You can use soft-drink cans if you cannot find any metal foil.

The metal foils used here are brass, copper, aluminum, and phosphorus bronze. Foils are very thin sheet metal. If you feel confident, draw the outline of your design directly onto the back of the metal with a soft pencil. Place the metal on a soft surface – an old magazine will do; now draw, pressing very heavily with a ballpoint pen over your pencil lines. Draw some freehand patterns – faces, stars, hearts, etc. – within the outline. Cut out the design with scissors and make a hole at the top for hanging.

Watch these metal shapes shine at night when the tree is all lit up.

LUMINOUS LEAVES

These lovely luminous metal leaves accented with glass beads create a beautiful shimmering effect dangling from the branches of the Christmas tree like enormous earrings.

Here are some precious-looking leaves to hang on your tree for a sparkling effect. Use the same types of metal foils that were used for the repoussé metal shapes described on pages 12-13. Cut some leaf shapes out of the metal foil and put them on a magazine. Make some leaf veins by pressing and rolling a tracing wheel across each one of the leaves.

Thread some brightly colored glass beads above and below the leaf with fine copper wire. The beads below the leaf help it to hang straight on the tree and contrast with the horizontal branches of pine needles.

A tree decorated solely with metal leaves, some with beads, some without, is a beautiful sight. The metal foil and beads sparkle in the reflected glow of electric Christmas tree lights.

You can make all the leaves with one type of metal foil as shown here, or you can try using several different types of foils. Choose the metals to match the style of your tree. Copper and bronze have a warmer feel to them; on the other hand, aluminum leaves accentuated with silver or pearl beads create a much cooler, more wintery effect.

You might like to experiment by painting some of the metal leaves with transparent glass paints (see Metal Menagerie pages 16-17).

Make a lovely garland for your tree by stringing the metal leaves together on a thin copper wire and interspersing them with glass beads.

These

shiny

metal leaves

make stunning

tree decorations.

Luminous leaves

can be made in a

great variety of

shapes and sizes

from several types

of metal foils.

METAL MENAGERIE

These charming little animals made from copper or aluminum foil are

inspired by the popular tin decorations from Mexico.

Transparent glass

paints can give an

extra sheen to a

colorful metal

menagerie.

Cut out simple animal shapes and draw patterns on the back with a ball-point pen.

Transparent glass paints can be used to good advantage on these metal figures; the metal sheen glimmering through the paint is very arresting. When the paint is thoroughly dry, you could try lightly rubbing the raised drawn lines with very fine sandpaper to reveal the glinting metal beneath.

The cornucopia, fish, and vase with flowers were made the same way and painted with opaque enamel paints. Matte or shiny paint can be used.

There are endless possibilities for these decorations; visit museums and galleries or look in art and craft books for inspiration.

HEAVENLY SHAPES

These simple shapes – moons, stars, and flowers – have been cut out of aluminum, bronze, and copper foil. There is very little repoussé work on the back; the glittering effect is created by adding flat-backed "jewels."

The crescent moon was edged from the back of the foil with a tracing wheel to create an even line of little raised dots on the front. Brightly colored "jewels" with different-sized facets were added to create a regal feel. Most clear adhesives are strong enough to hold the "jewels" in place.

This gold star has a large, imitation cut-diamond in the middle, surrounded by shimmering pearls.

The aluminum flower has a large jewel in the center with smaller ones on each petal to complement it.

The embellishments are your choice, depending on what is available.

Whatever you decide to use, the combination of the reflective metal and the glittering jewels is a winner.

MINIATURE MIRRORS & JEWELS

These miniature framed mirrors are inspired by Indian embroidery, in which lots of tiny mirrors are sewn onto a piece of fabric to give it a wonderfully rich and sparkling texture.

Cut the mirror frames out of the metal foil and draw some repoussé designs on the back, perhaps to frame the mirror or decorate the hanging tab.

The curly effect is produced by simply cutting the metal frame into very thin strips all around the outside. If the strips are cut thin enough, the metal will automatically curl into this unusual border. Stick your mirror onto the center of the frame with a strong epoxy glue. You can find small round, oval or rectangular mirrors where doll house miniatures are sold. Glue some little seed pearls or glass beads around the mirror to disguise the mirror's edge.

You may prefer to have a large jewel in the center of the frame instead of a mirror.

Try hanging these miniature mirrors on your lighted tree. Turn off the room lights and watch the mirrors throw their magical reflections around the darkened room.

The tiny mirrors in the center of these decorations add radiance and sparkle to any Christmas tree.

Metal figures can
be used in several
ways – as wreath
decorations, crib
figures, gift tags,
and, of course,
Christmas tree
ornaments.

METAL FIGURES

The man on the right and the woman on the opposite page are roughly based on images of seventeenth-century Pilgrims who founded the colony at Plymouth, Massachusetts.

You can really go to town working on the back of these metal figures with a dry ballpoint pen. Don't forget to pierce a hole in the top for suspending the little figures from the tree.

Why not make a whole family and their animals? What about Noah and his Ark? Or a nativity scene? The little angel at left could be one of your crib figures.

Metal figures look lovely pinned onto the front door at Christmas or perhaps attached to a festive wreath. Smaller figures could be made as gift tags, with the name of the recipient on each one. Remember you must write backwards so that the words will read correctly from the front.

This sturdy little character was given lots of interesting features by drawing on the back with a ballpoint pen.

EMBROIDERED BIRDS

What is more appropriate than to have a flock of birds settle on a tree? Perhaps these visitors have come from more exotic lands to brighten up our winters.

Bits of fabric can be fashioned into whimsical birds.

24

These unusual little birds, made from scraps of fabric and glittering ribbons, are embroidered with small seed beads and shining sequins. Little assorted packages of colorful sequins are readily available in most notions departments.

Use small pieces of fabric: the more exotic the better. Try gold lamé, shot silk, or diaphanous lace. Draw a very simple bird-shaped body onto a double thickness of fabric and cut it out slightly larger, taking the seam into account. Sew the pieces together, right sides facing, and leave a small opening for the padding. Turn right side out, fill with padding, and sew up the hole. Appliqué small contrasting bits of fabric for the wings, then embroider with beads and sequins. Add some ribbons. For the tails, you can use brightly colored feathers from feather dusters. Always make sure the eyes stand out.

The Scottish tartan bird with rhinestone eyes has a crown and tail made from the thin red ribbon that binds the body.

Gold tassels, small bells or a rich combination of beads hanging under the bird make an interesting addition.

The star and these little parcels are made from colorful fabrics and then embellished with bright ribbons and sequins.

SPARKLING STARS & PRECIOUS PARCELS

Stars hold a very special significance at Christmas. It was a gleaming star that led the Three Kings from far-off lands to the humble stable in Bethlehem. Stars hanging on our Christmas tree remind us of the star of Bethlehem.

These sparkling stars and precious little parcels are very easy to sew. Just cut out a star or parcel shape from a double thickness of fabric, remembering to add the seam allowance. Choose a variety of fabrics, perhaps ones that are richly patterned or have an antique look. You could also try shimmering and tinsel-like fabrics.

With the fabric right sides together, neatly sew around the shape, leaving a small opening. Turn the fabric right side out and stuff loosely. Insert a hanging loop before sewing up the opening.

Then go to town on the decorations, adding sequins and beads. Tie the parcels with colorful ribbons and bows. Cross the star with narrow ribbons and stud with starry sequins. Perhaps you could even add little jingle bells to each point of the star. Try hanging tassels from the three lower points of the star.

Tassels are easy to make. Simply wrap a small skein of metallic thread around your fingers, remove, and bind one end of the skein with the same thread. Cut the other end to form the tassel.

These delightful

ornaments are easy

to make; all you

need is some fabric

and glitter and lots

of imagination.

This richly

patterned red star

with its shiny gold

tassels would be a

lovely feature on

your Christmas

tree.

LUSCIOUS LEAVES & FLOWERS

These leaves and flowers are very easy to make and are so effective as Christmas ornaments. The pearly flower is made like a little cushion with a pleated silver ribbon edge. The gray silk center of the flower was decorated with a collection of old and new pearl buttons to signify seeds and then circled with a twinkling row of tiny pearls.

Use rich dark velvet to make the leaves. Cut a double layer of fabric into simple leaf shapes; be sure to include the seam allowances. Try using a contrasting color for the back of the leaf. With the right sides of the fabric facing together, sew around the leaf, leaving one end open. Turn right side out, stuff loosely, and, after inserting a hanging loop, sew up the open end. Use metallic thread to embroider the front with leaf veins. Pinpoint the ends of the veins with little seed pearls. As a variation, use long silvery beads to accentuate the leaf motif and finish with tiny iridescent seed beads. Finally, bind the hanging end of the leaves with matching metallic thread.

FROSTED FRUITS

These fruits were modeled in papier-mâché and allowed to dry thoroughly before being primed with a thick white primer and painted rich, ripe fruit colors. When the paint was dry, a little gold powder was dusted over the surface.

Those lovely tendrils on the grapes are easy to make from copper foil, which curls naturally when cut into thin strips.

Although ready-made pulp is available from craft or better toy stores, you may enjoy making your own from this recipe.

Tear a newspaper into small squares and, in an old pan, boil in plenty of water until the paper begins to disintegrate. Let cool, then mash with a potato masher. Drain off excess water and squeeze dry. Add half a cup of white glue, a sprinkling of dry wallpaper paste, half a cup of plaster-based filler and one cup of fine sawdust. Knead energetically until all the ingredients are well mixed. This pulp mixture will keep covered for a number of weeks in the refrigerator.

These little gold-dusted fruits are modeled out of papier-mâché pulp; the leaves are made from copper foil, which is pushed into the pulp fruit while it is still soft.

You could make a variety of fruit and create a riot of shimmering colors to decorate your tree.

BRILLIANT BIRDS

These brilliantly painted birds are modeled from papier-mâché pulp (see page 29), and, as with the frosted fruit, the metal wings and crowns are inserted into the pulp before it begins to dry. Remember to make a hole through the bird at this stage to accommodate a hanging loop.

The metal foil can be folded like a fan, cut into strips or tightly curled. For an unusual effect you can hold the metal crown and tail over a bare flame for a moment so that they take on a burnished patina. The pretty, white bird shown above has a tail and crown made from an unraveled aluminum scouring pad.

When the pulp is thoroughly dry, prime the birds and then paint them with bright acrylic or gouache paints.

Finally, add colored glitter to make the birds sparkle on the tree.

These bright little papier-mâché birds are adorned with metallic crowns and tails.

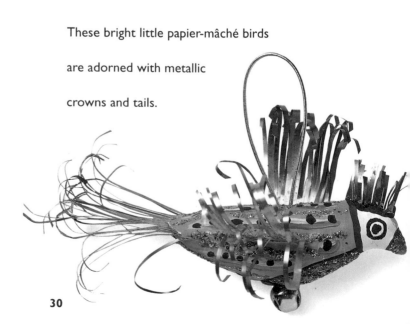

Try putting a little rider or acrobat on the horse, or make a sleigh for the reindeer to pull.

LITTLE PAINTED ANIMALS

These charming little animals are inspired by carved and

painted wooden toys made in India.

Start by making an internal framework of pipe cleaners and attach it to a cardboard base with strong glue. Model papier-mâché pulp (see page 29) around the framework to create an animal form – a horse, a fox, or a reindeer. Insert a little loop of wire into the back of the animal and cover the base with pasted newspaper strips. After it is thoroughly dry and primed, paint the animals in the manner of naive folk art, sometimes leaving the white primer to show as a contrast to the bright color. Add patterns, dots, and stripes, using colors that clash or dazzle.

These decorations employ the

most commonly used method of

making papier-mâché.

PARTY POPPERS, STOCKINGS, & CROWNS

First, cut the shapes from thin cardboard and carefully cover them all over with pasted newspaper. Remember to insert a small wire hook at this stage. When the paper is dry, prime the pieces and paint them with bright colors. Glue on some glittering wrapping paper or candy wrappers.

Motifs from a gold doily enhance the red and gold theme of the Christmas party poppers shown above.

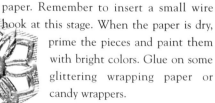

The majestic gold

crown in the

window looks

splendid with its

twinkling jewels;

gold glitter around

the edge finishes it

off in style.

Engraving on

painted ornaments

produces some

intriguing designs

with a very

professional look.

Engraved ornaments are a real pleasure to make. First wrap Styrofoam® balls with two layers of pasted paper. Let dry, then prime with two coats of white primer. Push a chopstick into one end of the ball to provide a handle and then start painting the ball with some brightly colored designs. When you remove the stick, the hole can be filled with glue to hold the hanging loop, which is a piece of gold pipe cleaner threaded with a bright glass bead.

When the paint is dry, add some finer details to your designs by carefully scratching out a pattern to reveal the white primer beneath the paint. Use a sharp pointed instrument, such as the blade of a mat-knife.

This engraving process is a traditional technique used in Switzerland to decorate Easter eggs. As you can see from the balls shown here, the final effect is very attractive and professional looking. People are always intrigued with these engraved ornaments and want to know how they were made.

PAINTED & ENGRAVED ORNAMENTS

These painted and engraved baubles make a spirited change from the traditional

glass balls that usually hang on the Christmas tree.

Save your Christmas gift wrapping paper and use it to make next year's ornaments. This is one of the quickest and most rewarding projects in the book.

ORNAMENTS GALORE

The continuous surface of a sphere provides an enormous canvas for decorating ideas.

To make these colorful and decorative ornaments, first paper some Styrofoam® balls with an array of different background colors. Then, using old bits of wrapping paper, candy wrappers, sequins, pearl-headed pins, glitter, some metallic thread and lots of imagination, make a whole range of dazzling ornaments. You could try some of the various techniques used to make the ornaments shown here. Dot the ball with flower-shaped sequins, securing them with small pearl-headed pins. Découpage motifs can be cut out of beautiful hand-printed papers. To add glittering silver stars; first paint some glue stars on the ball and then sprinkle them with glitter. Foil candy wrappers cut into strips are ideal for creating glittering striped balls. Bits of torn-up shiny paper can be glued between the stripes for added interest. Try binding some metallic thread over natural handmade papers or over crushed colored tissue paper.

There is no end to the variety of attractive ornaments you can make using odd bits of paper and some glittery embellishments.

MINIATURE CHURCH & HOUSES

These are buildings straight out of a fairy tale. Try making a whole village or the witch's cottage from the story of Hansel and Gretel.

These buildings are very simple to assemble from thin pieces of cardboard. The ones shown here were made from pizza boxes.

Look for ideas and inspiration in magazines, picture books, and especially travel catalogs. Make a simple house shape by sticking the cardboard together with white glue; use small strips of masking tape to hold the cardboard pieces in place while the glue dries, then paste thin paper all over the little building. Allow it to dry, then prime and paint with bright colors. Add sequins, glitter, and fine braid to finish.

This miniature church and the quaint little houses are modeled on decorative buildings of Eastern Europe.

DAZZLING DANGLES

These dazzling

dangles are

modeled out of

papier-mâché.

The glittering

jewels in the

center are added

while the pulp

base is still soft

and moist.

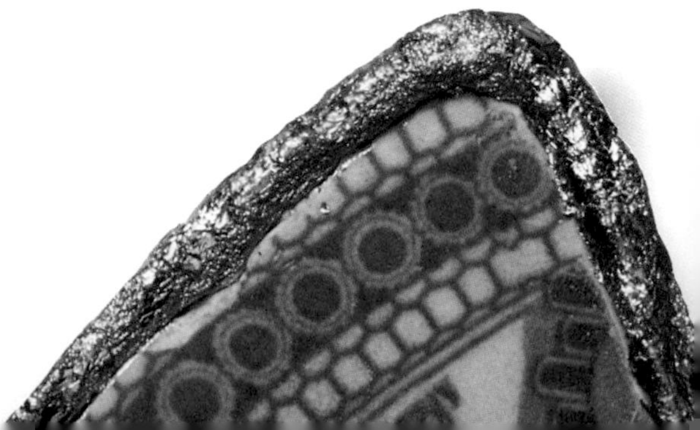

Model some stars, crescents, diamonds, hearts, and circles from papier-mâché pulp. While they are still soft, push a large, flat-backed faceted jewel into the center of each shape. The paper pulp will conveniently shrink a little when drying and hold the jewel firmly in place.

You can use any type of costume jewelry to make these dangles. This would be a good use for those old pieces of costume jewelry that you no longer wear. Anything that glitters will make a lovely center-piece for your ornaments.

Broken antique blue and white china shards can also be used instead of jewels. The dangles shown here were made with bits of eighteenth-century English china. The eccentric shape of the shard will dictate the way the pulp is modeled around it.

While the pulp is still soft, pierce a hole in it for the hanging loop. If you want to string a few of the dangles together, add little loops of wire at the top and bottom of each shape to keep them from sliding into one another. If they are to hang singly, then just one loop at the top of the dangle will do.

When the pulp is dry, carefully paint around the china or jewel with gold paint. For a really lustrous effect, add precious-metal leaf on top. You can buy books of silver, gold, copper, aluminum, or even patinated metal leaf quite inexpensively. It sticks readily to varnish that is just tacky and nearly dry. The final effect can be quite stunning.

Using odd bits of broken china adds interesting textures and shapes.

BEADS, BELLS, & BOWS

These stylish, elegant decorations are quick and

simple to make, but you need to be bold and

extravagant.

Use large beads and chandelier-type drop crystals for these tree ornaments. The ones shown here are made with a combination of large Indian pressed-metal beads and imitation crystals, which come in a range of colors and are much less expensive than glass crystals.

Figure out your color scheme carefully, perhaps adding little glass beads of a contrasting color between the crystal and metal beads. It is best to use thin copper or silver wire for threading; this is available in craft or bead shops. Complete your decorations with an elegant flourish, such as a matching bow at the top of the beads.

RADIANT RINGS

Decorative hoops

embellished with

beads and bows,

are an interesting

variation on hanging glass beads.

You can buy hoops or wire rings from jewelry suppliers or bead shops, or simply make your own from silver wire. Hang a combination of pressed metal and glittering glass beads from the bottom of the ring.

To make the ribbon rings, first pad the wire ring with polyester, creating some thickness, then tightly wrapping it with ribbon.

The ribbon ring on the right was finished with a pink organdy bow that picks up the iridescence in the crystal beads. The other two rings have gleaming gold bows to accent their blue and gold theme.

You could also try

threading beads

onto the wire ring

as shown below.

LARGE BEADED TASSELS

This golden tassel

was designed for a

large, boldly

decorated

Christmas tree.

Gold tassels have an opulent and palatial feel

about them, and these simple beaded tassels

have a glorious effect. Yet, both are deceptively

simple to make.

Try making a more unusual tassel, like the one shown opposite in gauzy lilac organdy. It is tightly bound at the top with gold thread, and threaded above with gold beads. A beautiful bronze ruched ribbon, tipped with a modest lilac bow, gives an elegant finishing touch.

The large tassel shown on the left is suspended from a gold-sprayed ball flecked with gold leaf. A rosette of metallic woven ribbon tops it off beautifully.

SHELL ORNAMENTS

The natural world is full of inspiration for the artist. What object could have more exquisite perfection and beauty than a seashell, with its extraordinary spiral forms and the natural iridescence of its pearly surface? The tree ornaments shown on these pages use teardrop pearls, beads, and ribbons to accentuate the natural beauty and charm of seashells.

Seashell ornaments shimmer in the light.

48

Shell ornaments are ideal for the sophisticated tree with pale, subtle colors. Use them with white, silver, or pearly decorations, and your tree will take on an otherworldly quality.

Collect interesting shells from the beach or buy them in gift or specialty shell shops (they are generally inexpensive). If you buy shells, choose common varieties that are not endangered.

Seashells are quite soft, so it is easy to drill little holes into them with a small awl or drill. Suspend teardrop pearls, silver stars, crystals, silver lockets, or little bunches of bells from silver wire threaded through the holes. Use ruched ribbons or polka-dot netting to complete the decoration.

49

NUTS & SEEDS

Nuts,

pine cones,

seed heads, and

cinnamon sticks

make naturally

beautiful

ornaments.

The incredible world of nature offers a wealth of intricate design. Walnuts, which are of course already designed to hang from a tree, are even more beautiful when sprayed gold or silver.

To embellish the natural design of nuts and seed heads, hang little metal charms beneath them. You could also quarter a walnut with shining red braid and top it with a matching plume of brightly colored feathers for a whimsical touch.

Alternatively, cut a walnut in half, scoop out the nut, and line the inside with luscious fabric. Then glue a gleaming jewel in the center and little seed pearls around the edge to accent the natural heart shape. Hang the nut shell from the tree with red braid attached with a little bow.

50

Spray a pine cone gold and top it with a gold bow and hanging loop. Or you could try painting the cones red or green and then adding glitter to the tips. Finish them with little tartan ribbon rosettes and matching braid hanging loops.

A poppy seed head makes an ideal Christmas tree ornament. Spray it gold, then pierce a little hole in the stem and fill it with glue. Insert a hanging loop that has been threaded with one or two glistening glass beads.

A little bunch of cinnamon sticks tied together with gold braid and a tassel is very evocative of the winter season.

When out on country walks, look for interesting nuts and seeds that you could use for tree decorations. With an inventive mind and creative combinations, the variety of ornaments you can make is limitless.

A cinnamon stick ornament gives off a delicious scent.

POMANDERS

Everybody knows of the Elizabethan pomander — an orange,

preserved and studded with spicily scented cloves. But there are

many alternatives to this old favorite.

Some are very simple to make,

and they are all quite

lovely.

These pomanders

could be scented

with a spicy

Christmas pot-

pourri essence.

For the shell pomander, quarter a Styrofoam® ball with gold ribbon and attach the tiny seashells with white glue inside each quarter. To help keep the shells in place while the glue is drying, make a little fence of dressmaking pins around the inside edge of the ribbon that defines the quarter you are working on. For neatness, attach all the shells in one direction. When the ball is completely covered, make a rosette with the same type of ribbon, then push the rosette and a hanging loop into a small glue-filled hole at the top of the pomander.

The rosebud and white helicrysum pomanders couldn't be simpler. Just push the pointed dried flower stems into a foam ball.

SALT DOUGH

Salt dough is another traditional favorite for

Christmas decorations. And it is

particularly suitable for children, as

long as they don't try to eat it!

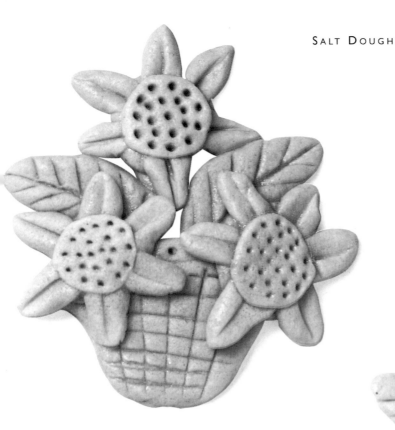

Salt-dough

ornaments can

be left in their

natural state or

painted with

vibrant colors.

The basic recipe for salt dough is 2 cups of all-purpose flour and 1 cup of salt. Add water gradually to the dry ingredients until the mixture is stiff, but not sticky, then knead for about ten minutes until it is smooth and manageable.

Working on a floured board, shape wreaths, hearts and baskets of flowers out of the dough. Use bits of dough to add interesting details and embellishments. Make a hole through the top of the dough figure for threading a ribbon, or just glue the ribbon onto the back.

When you have made your shapes, allow them to dry thoroughly for a few days. A warm oven may help for a short time, but take care not to cook them or they will yellow.

Varnish some of the shapes in their natural color. Paint others with vivid colors to look like South American salt-dough decorations. Varnish these as well to enhance the color.

CHRISTMAS COOKIES

Every Christmas, celebrants make delicious spicy cookies in great abundance to give to visitors during the holiday season. Cookies can also be used as festive Christmas tree decorations.

Tie some cookies onto the tree with pretty ribbons or to keep them really fresh, bunch a few cookies in a cellophane package and tie it onto the tree.

There are many flavors and shapes of Christmas cookies: wreath-shaped aniseed cookies; cinnamon and almond cookies cut into simple shapes and iced before baking for a glazed effect; jelly-filled shortbread sandwiches with a hole in the top layer to reveal the jelly center. Try adapting your favorite recipes to create some interesting variations. Cut out the cookies in different shapes — stars, hearts, diamonds, Christmas trees. Try the Swiss technique of pressing the dough into molds, creating relief pictures.

GARLANDS

Garlands provide a wonderful contrast to vertically hung

decorations. A tree lavishly swagged and

looped with glorious garlands is a spectacle

to behold. Here are some ideas to spark

your imagination.

Garlands can be

made with everyday

objects such as

scouring pads and

packing chips.

Gold and silver

paint or sequins

produce some

stunning effects.

Golden ribbons and glass beads create an exquisite-looking garland for your Christmas tree.

Unravel a silver or copper scouring pad and press in little pink and red sequin stars. You might want to use dried flowers or little shells instead of sequins. One pad will stretch for about a yard, so you may need a few to decorate a tree.

Here is a way to put Styrofoam® packing chips to good use. Spray them gold and silver and thread them together in an interesting pattern, then loop the garland around your tree for a spectacular effect.

For a softer look, sew together a length of golden ribbon bows. You can sew little glass beads between the bows.

Chinese lanterns make a colorful garland. String the lanterns together with thin copper wire or nylon string, threading shells and beads in between each lantern.

TREE BASE

Whether you have a potted or a cut Christmas tree, you will

need some way of treating the base to complement the

riot of festive decorations that adorn it.

Your live tree may come already planted in a pot. If not, plant it firmly in a generous-sized pot; clay or plastic will do equally well. If you are using a cut tree, line a pot with a plastic bag, wedge the tree securely with logs, and pour sand in the pot to make it solid.

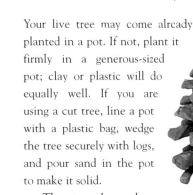

The tree base shown here, was made by decorating a straight-sided basket large enough to hold the pot. The basket was first sprayed silver and then spatter sprayed with gold paint to give it a rich gold and silver effect. Crushed iridescent paper was arranged loosely on top of the flower pot around the tree trunk to create a really sumptuous base for the tree. Two wired ribbons with luscious bows tied at the front were wrapped around the basket.

Wired ribbon can easily be pushed into shape and stays in place on the basket. The purple ribbon with its gold trim is a perfect complement to the gold-flecked basket and the iridescent paper.

The charm of a well-decorated tree begins at the base. A basket tree container can be beautifully decorated to tie in with the overall theme of the rest of your tree.

61

TREE TOPPERS

Crowning the top of the Christmas

tree is the climax of all your tree

decorating achievements.

A star is the traditional

tree topper. Here are some

ideas for stars that will top your

richly decorated tree with a

spectacular flourish.

To make your Christmas tree star, start by cutting the basic star shape out of a thick piece of cardboard. Model the faceted sides of the star with paper pulp (see page 29). Do this on both sides of the cardboard base. While the paper pulp is still soft and moist, insert a substantial piece of wire into one of the points of the star; curl the wire into a loose spiral. This will hold your star on the topmost branch of the tree. When the pulp is thoroughly dry, paper over the star.

You can embellish your star in a variety of ways to match the general theme of your Christmas tree. The star on the left was decorated with subtly contrasting, glittery candy wrappers that emphasize the faceted points of the star.

The star on the right was primed with two coats of white primer and a base color of terra cotta. The surface of the star was rubbed all over with silver gilt cream and then polished to a gleaming sheen. For a finishing touch, the points of the star were punctuated with teardrop pearls.

A star provides a stylish finish to your Christmas tree. This delicate silvery star with its pearldrop points would look stunning atop a sparkling wintry tree hung with white, silver and pearl decorations.

ACKNOWLEDGMENTS

The author would like to thank Ïenella Brown for her contributions to this book on p.16, pp.18–19, p.26 (little parcels), p.29, pp.34–35, pp.38–39 (some of the ornaments), p.44 (beaded bow, left), p.45 (ring, left), p.46, p.52 (rosebud pomander), pp.58–59 (gold and silver garland, ribbon and bow garland). She would also like to thank Heini Schneebeli for his lovely, clear photographs.